FRESH ENCO

A Plumb Line for God's People

Henry T. Blackaby & Claude V. King

LifeWay Press

Nashville, Tennessee

© Copyright 1993 • LifeWay Press
All rights reserved

7200-03

Dewey Decimal Classification: 248.4
Subject Heading: Christian Life/Discipleship

Unless otherwise indicated, Scripture quotations are from
The Holy Bible, *New International Version*, copyright ©
1973, 1978, 1984 by International Bible Society.

Printed in the United States of America

LifeWay Press
127 Ninth Avenue, North
Nashville, Tennessee 37234

Contents

Introduction to A Plumb Line for God's People

THE PARABLE OF THE LEANING TOWER OF PISA • A
bell tower was built in Pisa, Italy, between 1174 and
1350. The tower is 177 feet tall with marble walls
between six and thirteen feet wide. The ground beneath
the tower was not solid enough to support the weight of
the tower, and it began to sink on one side. The tower
leans more than 17 feet off center. Today it is considered
one of the Seven Wonders of the Modern World.

◆ Where do you think the primary problem exists with
the leaning tower? Check one.
❏ The problem is with the walls. If they were straight-
   ened, everything would be fine.
❏ The problem is with the foundation. If the foundation
   were firm and in line, the walls would be straight as well.

If a huge crane could straighten the walls, the problem
would still exist when the tower was released. Without a
solid foundation the tower will remain crooked.

In a similar way, your spiritual life has its foundation in a
love relationship with God. The way you live your life,
practice your faith, and obey God's commands can be
represented by the tower. If your life is out of line with
God's plan, the problem is in your love relationship.

Jesus said, "He who does not love me will not obey my
teaching," but "if anyone loves me, he will obey my
teaching" (John 14:24,23).

GOD'S INVITATION: RETURN TO YOUR FIRST LOVE • In
His first letter to the churches in Revelation, the risen
Christ extended an invitation. Most of us need to hear and
respond to it. The letter was to the church in Ephesus.
Jesus commended their hard work, their perseverance, and
their intolerance of evil. Yet they had a fatal flaw.

6

⁴"Yet I hold this against you: You have forsaken your first love. ⁵Remember the height from which you have fallen! Repent and do the things you did at first. If you do not repent, I will come to you and remove your lampstand from its place. . . . ⁷To him who overcomes, I will give the right to eat from the tree of life, which is in the paradise of God."

—Revelation 2:4-7

God's invitation is for us to repent and return to our first love. Christ's word to the church at Ephesus indicates that failure to repent is fatal. Christ said He would remove their lampstand if they refused to return to their first love—God. If we fail to return to our first love, we will miss out on the abundant life God intends for His people.

GOD'S PLUMB LINE • In Scripture, God uses the plumb line to describe what He is doing with His people:

⁷"This is what he showed me: The Lord was standing by a wall that had been built true to plumb, with a plumb line in his hand. ⁸And the Lord asked me, "What do you see, Amos?"

"A plumb line," I replied.

Then the Lord said, "Look, I am setting a plumb line among my people Israel; I will spare them no longer."

—Amos 7:7-8

As God's people, we are to be like a straight wall—true to plumb. When we depart from God, we fail to realize how far we have departed. We often don't understand how seriously we have strayed from God. We may not realize how close we are to collapse or destruction. To guide us, God uses a plumb line to help us see how far we have departed.

God's Word reveals God Himself, His purposes and ways. The Scriptures serve as God's plumb line for us. When we see that we have departed from His ideals, purposes, ways, and commands, we can know clearly that we have a problem. We have left our love relationship with Him. We cannot love God correctly unless we obey Him. It is spiritually impossible. If we are not obeying

God, it is because we do not love Him with all our hearts (Read John 14:15-26).

Revival • Genuine revival does not come simply by reforming our behavior. Just changing our ways is not sufficient. Unless our love relationship with God is repaired, we will eventually go back to our old ways of living. The only lasting motivation for obedience to God is a sound love relationship with Him. If our love relationship with God is right, our lives will line up with His standards and His covenant of love with His people.

◆ In your spiritual life which of the following leads to genuine revival?

❏ A change in my behavior. If I get my act together, then my relationship with God will be restored.
❏ A change in my love relationship with God. If I get my love relationship with God corrected, then I will change my behavior because I love Him.

Do you see the connection? A right love relationship with God is a requirement for genuine revival. Correct behavior comes because of the love relationship. To reform behavior without a change in the relationship with God is temporary and superficial. Revival requires a change of heart and a change of life.

Revival means to restore or renew life. Revival is for God's people who need a fresh encounter, a fresh love relationship with Him. Revival is God using the plumb line of His Word. God calls us as His people to repent and return to a holy love relationship with Him. When we repent and return to God, our hearts return to Him. God forgives and cleanses. God restores life. This is revival. God gives renewed life. For God is our life (Deut. 30:19-20; John 14:6; 1 John 5:11-12).

GOD'S PROMISE • Second Chronicles 7:13-14 tells what is necessary for revival and spiritual awakening:

> [13]"When I shut up the heavens so that there is no rain, or command locusts to devour the

land or send a plague among my people, [14]if my people, who are called by my name, will humble themselves and pray and seek my face and turn from their wicked ways, then will I hear from heaven and will forgive their sin and will heal their land."

The healing of our nation is waiting for the repentance of God's people. For the sake of God's glory, because of His love, to honor His Son Jesus in His body—the church, for the sake of our children and relatives, for the sake of our neighbors and friends, for the healing of our nation . . . let us, as God's chosen people humble ourselves, pray, cry out to Him and seek His face, turn from our wicked ways, and return to our love relationship with Jesus.

[1]"Come, all you who are thirsty" . . . [6]Seek the Lord while he may be found; call on him while he is near. [7]Let the wicked forsake his way and the evil man his thoughts. Let him turn to the Lord, and he will have mercy on him, and to our God, for he will freely pardon. . . .

[11]"So is my word that goes out from my mouth: It will not return to me empty, but will accomplish what I desire and achieve the purpose for which I sent it. [12]You will go out in joy and be led forth in peace; the mountains and hills will burst into song before you, and all the trees of the field will clap their hands."
—Isaiah 55:1,6-7,11-12

YOUR PASTOR'S ROLE

God wants to work through pastors to bring about a sweeping revival that will last for an extended time—perhaps a generation. God has given your church a pastor or shepherd. God holds your pastor accountable for the leadership and shepherding of His people. Your pastor will be in prayer and in God's Word to provide the spiritual leadership your church needs. Consider Acts 6:1-7.

¹In those days when the number of disciples was increasing, the Grecian Jews among them complained against the Hebraic Jews because their widows were being overlooked in the daily distribution of food. ²So the Twelve gathered all the disciples together and said, "It would not be right for us to neglect the ministry of the word of God in order to wait on tables. ³Brothers, choose seven men from among you who are known to be full of the Spirit and wisdom. We will turn this responsibility over to them ⁴and will give our attention to prayer and the ministry of the word."

⁵This proposal pleased the whole group. They chose Stephen, a man full of faith and of the Holy Spirit; also Philip, Procorus, Nicanor, Timon, Parmenas, and Nicolas from Antioch, a convert to Judaism. ⁶They presented these men to the apostles, who prayed and laid their hands on them.

⁷So the word of God spread. The number of disciples in Jerusalem increased rapidly, and a large number of priests became obedient to the faith.

Be sensitive to ways you can encourage your pastor to be the spiritual leader your church needs. As a church body, free your pastor to become a man of prayer and a man of God's Word as the church in Jerusalem did (Acts 6:3-4).

God has also given other leaders to assist your pastor in this responsibility. Your pastor and the leaders of your church will be seeking to guide you, as God's people.

Be in prayer for your pastor and church leaders. Ask God to guide them with wisdom, knowledge, and power. Pray that God will give them a clear indication of when and how to lead the church body to return to God. Be patient and trust God to guide your church leaders.

Prayers

PRAYER OF REVIVAL: PSALM 85:4-9

[4]Restore us again, O God our Savior, and put away your displeasure toward us. [5]Will you be angry with us forever? Will you prolong your anger through all generations? [6]Will you not revive us again, that your people may rejoice in you? [7]Show us your unfailing love, O Lord, and grant us your salvation. [8]I will listen to what God the Lord will say; he promises peace to his people, his saints—but let them not return to folly. [9]Surely his salvation is near those who fear him, that his glory may dwell in our land.

PRAYER OF PREPARATION: PSALM 139

[1]O Lord, you have searched me and you know me. [2]You know when I sit and when I rise; you perceive my thoughts from afar. [3]You discern my going out and my lying down; you are familiar with all my ways. [4]Before a word is on my tongue you know it completely, O Lord.

[5]You hem me in—behind and before; you have laid your hand upon me. [6]Such knowledge is too wonderful for me, too lofty for me to attain.

[7]Where can I go from your Spirit? Where can I flee from your presence? [8]If I go up to the heavens, you are there; if I make my bed in the depths, you are there. [9]If I rise on the wings of the dawn, if I settle on the far side of the sea, [10]even there your hand will guide me, your right hand will hold me fast.

[11]If I say, "Surely the darkness will hide me and the light become night around me," [12]even the darkness will not be dark to you; the night will shine like the day, for darkness is as light to you.

[13]For you created my inmost being; you knit me together in my mother's womb. [14]I praise you because I am fearfully and wonderfully made. . . . [16]All the days ordained for me were written in your book before one of them came to be.

[17]How precious to me are your thoughts, O God!

[23]Search me, O God, and know my heart; test me and know my anxious thoughts. [24]See if there is any offensive way in me, and lead me in the way everlasting.

Spiritual Blessings Litany
Ephesians 1:3 - 14

LEADER: Praise be to the God and Father of our Lord Jesus Christ, who has blessed us in the heavenly realms with every spiritual blessing in Christ.

MEN: For he chose us in him before the creation of the world to be holy and blameless in his sight.

WOMEN: In love he predestined us to be adopted as his sons through Jesus Christ, in accordance with his pleasure and will—

ALL: To the praise of his glorious grace, which he has freely given us in the One he loves.

LEADER: In him we have redemption through his blood, the forgiveness of sins,

MEN: in accordance with the riches of God's grace that he lavished on us with all wisdom and understanding.

LEADER: He made known to us the mystery of his will according to his good pleasure, which he purposed in Christ,

WOMEN: to be put into effect when the times will have reached their fulfillment—to bring all things in heaven and on earth together under one head, even Christ.

ALL: In him we were also chosen,

LEADER: having been predestined according to the plan of him who works out everything in conformity with the purpose of his will,

ALL: in order that we, who were the first to hope in Christ, might be for the praise of his glory.

MEN: You also were included in Christ when you heard the word of truth, the gospel of your salvation.

WOMEN: Having believed, you were marked in him with a seal, the promised Holy Spirit,

ALL: who is a deposit guaranteeing our inheritance until the redemption of those who are God's possession—to the praise of his glory.

God's Standard for the Family

The following standards are drawn directly from Scripture. Because the world has so influenced our thinking and practice related to family life, the Scriptures may be in sharp contrast to your own family life. You may find yourself using human reason to explain why God's Word is no longer valid for today. You may find yourself trying to argue with God about His standards for the family. Both of these human-centered responses are good indicators that your heart may have shifted. Keep in mind that many of the problems faced by families today are the direct consequences of refusal to live by God's standards for family life.

You must decide whether to believe God or the counsel of the world concerning standards for family life. Before going further, pray that God will clearly guide you and your family in right living no matter what the cost.

MESSAGE NOTES: GOD'S STANDARD FOR THE FAMILY

- No part of life today is feeling the incredible hurt of departing from God's pattern more than the family.

- The hurt and brokenness in families in the church is as prevalent as the hurt and brokenness in families outside the church.

- God is saying, When I called you to be a people of mine and put you here, the way in which I want that covenant relationship with me to work itself out into succeeding generations is through the family.

- The family unit is the center of God's purpose of having His people continue in an experience of joining Him on His redemptive mission.

- The connection between the love relationship with God and how that love relationship is to be implemented in and through the family is found in Deuteronomy 6:4-9.

Deuteronomy 6:4-9 • [4]Hear, O Israel: The Lord our God, the Lord is one. [5]Love the Lord your God with all your heart and with all your soul and with all your strength. [6]These commandments that I give you today are to be upon your hearts. [7]Impress them on your children. Talk about them when you sit at home and when you walk along the road, when you lie down and when you get up. [8]Tie them as symbols on your hands and bind them on your foreheads. Write them on the doorframes of your houses and on your gates.

• The key to a nation rests on the strength of its family life, and that is particularly true of God's people.

PSALM 78:1-8

[1]O my people, hear my teaching;
    listen to the words of my mouth.
[2]I will open my mouth in parables,
    I will utter hidden things, things from of
    old—
[3]what we have heard and known,
    what our fathers have told us.
[4]We will not hide them from their children;
    we will tell the next generation
the praiseworthy deeds of the Lord,
    his power, and the wonders he has done.
[5]He decreed statutes for Jacob
    and established the law in Israel,
which he commanded our forefathers
    to teach their children,
[6]so the next generation would know them,
    even the children yet to be born,
    and they in turn would tell their children.
[7]Then they would put their trust in God
    and would not forget his deeds
    but would keep his commands.
[8]They would not be like their forefathers—
    a stubborn and rebellious generation,

> whose hearts were not loyal to God,
> whose spirits were not faithful to him.

There is no substitute for parents in carrying out these commands given in Scripture.

• The intimate and permanent covenant relationship in marriage is reflected in the covenant relationship of God with His people.

• God said to us, Don't marry outside the relationship with God.

• No plague threatens God's eternal purpose for His people more than divorce. God hates divorce.

> **MALACHI 2:13-16** • [13]You flood the Lord's altar with tears. You weep and wail because he no longer pays attention to your offerings or accepts them with pleasure from your hands. [14]You ask, "Why?" It is because the Lord is acting as the witness between you and the wife of your youth, because you have broken faith with her, though she is your partner, the wife of your marriage covenant.
>
> [15]Has not the Lord made them one? In flesh and spirit they are his. And why one? Because he was seeking godly offspring. So guard yourself in your spirit, and do not break faith with the wife of your youth. [16]"I hate divorce," says the Lord God of Israel, "and I hate a man's covering himself with violence as well as with his garment," says the Lord Almighty.
>
> So guard yourself in your spirit, and do not break faith.

• Why is God so opposed to the breakup of the family? God is looking for a seed to carry out His purpose to redeem a world.

• God never intended for a family to function without the corporate strength and help of the church family.

- The heart cry of the righteous over family life today is reflected in Jeremiah 8:21—9:1.

  "Since my people are crushed, I am crushed; I mourn, and horror grips me. Is there no balm in Gilead? Is there no physician there? Why then is there no healing for the wound of my people? Oh, that my head were a spring of water and my eyes a fountain of tears! I would weep day and night for the slain of my people."

- The church is people who feel what is happening in family life, strengthen it, change it, and bring all their resources to bear upon it.

- What would happen in our land today if the world stood and watched the incredible power of Almighty God healing family after family after family?

- No greater redemptive work could be done in our nation today than for the world to see the incredible power of God creating healthy, wholesome, powerful family lives with Christ as the center. God could draw thousands of families to say, "Whatever you are doing, I want it to happen in my family also." A church can surround families, when marriage has been broken, with God's pattern not only for marriage but restoration. When we do, this can be one of the greatest challenges for revival to happen.

May God draw us back to His plumb line for family life that He might bring great revival and spiritual awakening across our land.

QUESTIONS FOR GOD'S PEOPLE

1. Have we departed from God's plumb line regarding marriage and family life? How have we departed?
2. What difference does the world see in the lives of the couples and families of our church?
3. Are we providing support for healthy marriages and healthy families? What are we doing?
4. Are we doing things that hinder, hurt, or conflict with healthy family life? What?

5. What does God want to do through us to strengthen marriages?
6. What does God want to do through us to strengthen families?
7. Are there couples or families that we need to surround with love, prayer, and support to help rescue their marriage or family? Who?
8. How can we help each other be all God wants us to be for His glory?
9. How can we mobilize prayer support for couples and families?

The following is an expansion of what was presented on the videotape. Use these to reflect on God's standard for the family.

MARRIAGE AND SINGLES
MATTHEW 19:4-6
MATTHEW 19:10-12
2 CORINTHIANS 6:14-15,17
1 CORINTHIANS 7:1-9
HEBREWS 13:4-5

QUESTIONS FOR GOD'S PEOPLE
1. Are we as a church upholding God's ideal for marriage regarding permanence and marriage partners' being believers?
2. Are we honoring marriage by upholding purity for marriage partners? (Heb. 13:4.)
3. Are we dealing with people according to Scriptures who are sexually immoral? (1 Cor. 5.)

QUESTIONS FOR SINGLES
4. Does God want me to marry or remain single? Which life-style will allow me to better devote myself to His kingdom work?
5. Am I able to control my passions or should I seek marriage to avoid sexual immorality?
6. Am I in a relationship leading toward marriage that is out of line with God's plumb line?

7. Are we fulfilling our marital duty to one another (1 Cor. 7:3-5)?
8. Are we keeping our marriage bed pure from all sexual immorality and adultery?
9. Are we free from the love of money and the things of the world? Are we content with the things we have?

DIVORCE
MATTHEW 19:3-12
MATTHEW 5:31-32
LUKE 16:18
1 CORINTHIANS 7:10-16

QUESTIONS FOR CONSIDERATION

1. Has our church departed from God's plumb line regarding the permanence of marriage?
2. Do the number of divorces in our church family indicate that we have failed to strengthen marriages and uphold God's standards for marriage?
3. What are we doing to help couples experience the power of God in reconciling their marriages?
4. What are we doing to help divorced persons be reconciled with God? Are we helping them return to God's plumb line?
5. Have you divorced? If so, have you experienced the forgiveness of the Lord? Is reconciliation possible if neither you nor your spouse has remarried?
6. Are you considering divorce? Are you willing to humble yourself and seek the help of your church family in finding reconciliation?

PARENTS
PROVERBS 13:24
PROVERBS 22:6
PROVERBS 23:13-14
EPHESIANS 6:4
COLOSSIANS 3:21

QUESTIONS FOR PARENTS

1. Are you impressing God's teachings on your children? When you sit? walk? lie down? get up?

2. Does God's Word have a prominent place in your home?
3. Do you tell your children about God's praiseworthy deeds? His power? His wonders?
4. Do you provide firm discipline for your children in a spirit of love? Are you withholding discipline that is needed?
5. Do you exasperate (aggravate, anger, annoy, hassle, infuriate, irritate, pester, or provoke) or embitter your children?
6. Do you encourage and affirm your children?

HUSBANDS AND WIVES

These Scriptures relate to both husbands and wives. There are separate sections for each that follow.

> **1 PETER 2:11-13,15-17,21-25**
> **1 PETER 3:8-17**
> **EPHESIANS 5:21**

QUESTIONS FOR HUSBANDS AND WIVES

1. Are you abstaining from sinful desires?
2. How are your lives bringing glory to God as people observe the way you live?
3. Are you submitting yourselves to every authority over you? (1 Pet. 2:13)
4. How are you submitting yourselves to each other out of reverence for Christ? (Eph. 5:21) How are you showing respect for each other?
5. How are you responding in a godly way to suffering, insults, and threats? (1 Pet. 2:21-25)
6. Are you living in harmony with each other? How are you sympathetic, loving, compassionate, and humble toward each other?
7. How do you keep your tongue from evil and your lips from deceitful speech?
8. Have you made Christ Lord in your hearts?
9. Are you prepared to give an answer to people who ask you about the hope you have in Christ? What is your answer?

HUSBANDS

1 PETER 3:7
EPHESIANS 5:25-33
MALACHI 4:5-6

QUESTIONS FOR HUSBANDS

1. Are you considerate of your wife?
2. How do you treat her with respect and protect her?
3. Do you treat her as an equal heir of the grace of God?
4. Are your prayers being hindered because you do not treat your wife as God instructs?
5. How are you loving your wife like Christ loved the church—giving yourself up for her? Are you loving her as much as you love your own body? As much as you love yourself?
6. How are you making sure she has her basic needs met? Are you caring for her needs?
7. Have you left father and mother in order to have the needed intimacy with your wife?
8. As a husband and father, do you have a heart toward your children so God can turn the hearts of your children toward Him and the family?

WIVES

1 PETER 3:1-6
EPHESIANS 5:22-24,33B

QUESTIONS FOR WIVES

1. How do you submit to your husband the way you do to the Lord?
2. Does your husband see purity or impurity in your life?
3. Does your husband see reverence or disrespect in your life?
4. Do you emphasize outward beauty—fine clothes, fancy hair styles, and expensive jewelry? Or do you emphasize inward beauty—a gentle and quiet spirit?
5. Is your spirit toward your husband gentle or harsh?
6. Is your spirit toward your husband quiet and peaceable or do you cause turmoil in his life?
7. How do you show respect for your husband?

CHILDREN
EPHESIANS 6:1-3

QUESTIONS FOR CHILDREN
1. How do you demonstrate obedience toward your parents out of reverence and obedience to Christ?
2. How do you honor and show respect to your parents?

A FAMILY REPENTS: GENESIS 34–35

The following is an account of a family that repented and returned to God. The role of the family leader was vital in this experience. As you read, see if God directs you to any action your family may need to take.

JACOB'S FAMILY SINS (GEN. 34:25-31) • Jacob's daughter was raped, and out of revenge Simeon and Levi deceived the Shechemites, killed every male in the city, plundered the city of all its wealth, and took the women and children. Jacob said: "You have brought trouble on me by making me a stench to the Canaanites and Perizzites, the people living in this land. We are few in number, and if they join forces against me and attack me, I and my household will be destroyed" (Gen. 34:30).

GOD INVITED JACOB TO RETURN TO HIM • Jacob had encountered God at Bethel. God instructed Jacob to return to Bethel to live and worship God: "Go up to Bethel and settle there, and build an altar there to God, who appeared to you when you were fleeing from your brother Esau" (Gen. 35:1).

JACOB CALLED HIS FAMILY TO REPENTANCE (GEN. 35:2-4) • Jacob (the father and spiritual leader of the household) called on all his household to give up their foreign gods, to purify themselves, and to change their clothes. The family obeyed. They gave up their foreign gods and the rings in their ears that symbolized their allegiance to another god. Jacob buried the icons and jewelry at Shechem to put an end to their idolatry.

GOD'S RESPONSE (GEN. 35:5-15) • "The terror of God fell upon the towns all around them so that no one pursued them" (Gen. 35:5). God gave them safety. Jacob worshiped God at Bethel, and God appeared to him again and blessed him changing his name from Jacob (he deceives) to Israel (he struggles with God). God renewed His covenant relationship with Abraham's descendants:

> God said to him, "I am God Almighty; be fruitful and increase in number. A nation and a community of nations will come from you, and kings will come from your body. The land I gave to Abraham and Isaac I also give to you, and I will give this land to your descendants after you."
>
> —Genesis 35:11-12

Jacob set up a spiritual (stone) marker to remember this encounter with God and called the place Bethel which means "house of God."

QUESTIONS FOR FAMILIES TO CONSIDER

1. Have we given first place to Christ in our family life? How or how not?
2. Is the love of Christ reflected in our relationships with one another?
3. Have we allowed our love for television, movies, pleasure, or material things to distract us from our love relationship with God?
4. Are there any "false gods"—either activities or things—that we need to get rid of? If so, what? and how?
5. How can we develop a closer relationship to God in our family?

Notes

Religion vs. Reality

• We lose the reality of God's presence when we begin to practice religion without the relationship with the God who saves us.

• Religion without relationship can be deadly.

• God pursues the love relationship.

• The Lord issues a heart cry through His Word to His people.

> **JAMES 4:8-10** • ⁸Come near to God and he will come near to you. Wash your hands, you sinners, and purify your hearts, you double-minded. ⁹Grieve, mourn and wail. Change your laughter to mourning and your joy to gloom. ¹⁰Humble yourselves before the Lord, and he will lift you up.

• God's presence will be so real in them and through them that He can touch a lost world.

• Religion without relationship can become fanatic and can destroy the work of God.

• When God is present, everything changes. You will know it!

• A church is a people in meaningful, personal relationship with Jesus Christ and with each other. They enter into relationship with one another and then watch to see how God will thrust them into His world-redemptive plan.

• Two problems we face as to why people turn to religion rather than relationship: (1) We are not making certain that people are born again by the Spirit of God. People don't want radical change. They want God as an additive, not One who transforms. (2) We are not helping people experience genuine repentance. Repentance involves a change of mind, heart, will, and action.

- How can the reality of the presence of God return to His people?

    1. For the individual, it may be to ask:
        a. Have I been born again by the Spirit of God?
            - Have I confessed that I am a sinner?
            - Have I agreed with God that Jesus' death on the cross and His resurrection from the dead are my only hope for salvation?
            - Have I asked God to forgive me of my sin and to cleanse me by Jesus' shed blood?
            - Have I surrendered my will and life to the lordship of Jesus Christ?
            - Have I received God's free gift of eternal life?

    Ask God to help you understand your true relationship with Him. According to Romans 8:16, "The Spirit himself testifies with our spirit that we are God's children."

        b. If so, what is the evidence that I have experienced the new birth?
            - Has Christ taken up residence in my life?
            - Is the Holy Spirit affirming me that I am God's child?
            - Do I hear God's voice (spiritually) and follow Him?
            - Do I love my brothers and sisters in Christ?
            - Does the Holy Spirit reveal spiritual truths to me?
            - Is God's power and presence evident in my life?
            - Is God producing spiritual fruit through my life?

2 Corinthians 5:17 • If anyone is in Christ, he is a new creation; the old has gone, the new has come!

Read the contrasts between the old nature and the new. Which one best describes you?

THE OLD SINFUL NATURE

GALATIANS 5:19-21 • [19]The acts of the sinful nature are obvious: sexual immorality, impurity and debauchery; [20]idolatry and witchcraft; hatred, discord, jealousy, fits of rage, selfish ambition, dissensions, factions [21]and envy; drunkenness, orgies, and the like. I warn you, as I did before, that those who live like this will not inherit the kingdom of God.

ROMANS 8:5,7-8 • [5]Those who live according to the sinful nature have their minds set on what that nature desires; but those who live in accordance with the Spirit have their minds set on what the Spirit desires. . . . [7]The sinful mind is hostile to God. It does not submit to God's law, nor can it do so. [8]Those controlled by the sinful nature cannot please God.

THE NEW LIFE IN THE SPIRIT

GALATIANS 5:22-24 • [22]The fruit of the Spirit is love, joy, peace, patience, kindness, goodness, faithfulness, [23]gentleness and self-control.

[24]Those who belong to Christ Jesus have crucified the sinful nature with its passions and desires.

ROMANS 8:9-10 • [9]You, however, are controlled not by the sinful nature but by the Spirit, if the Spirit of God lives in you. And if anyone does not have the Spirit of Christ, he does not belong to Christ. [10]But if Christ is in you, your body is dead because of sin, yet your spirit is alive because of righteousness.

2. A church would need to ask:
   a. Do we experience Christ as Head of this church?
   b. Do we sense His presence and guidance in all we do?
   c. What evidence is there in our church of the resurrection power of Christ?
   d. What is the evidence of God's presence being manifest?
3. A denomination would ask: What is the evidence of God in His reigning presence explosively touching a lost world for Christ through us?
4. Our nation would ask: Where is the blessing of God on our nation, turning our nation back to God (Isa. 1:5a,18-20)?

QUESTIONS FOR GOD'S PEOPLE

1. Do you have a desire to be on mission with God? Do you hear God's voice and follow Him obediently?
2. When you pray, do you get answers to your prayers? Have you stopped praying because you do not see any practical purpose in prayer?
3. When you read God's Word, do you sense that God is present and guiding you through His word? How does He reveal spiritual truth to you through His Word?
4. As my congregation participates in worship services, do we sense the power and presence of God? How?
5. Do our members understand spiritual truth? In what way is this evident?
6. Have we placed more emphasis on decisions rather than converts?
7. Do our members have a heart for God and His purposes? Do our members have a desire to do the will of God?
8. Do we sense and see unity in our church body because of the common bond we have in Christ? How do we show that we are one in heart, mind, and spirit?
9. Have you substituted religious activity for a love relationship with God? Have you really been born again by God's Spirit into that love relationship?

Notes

Substitutes for God

Many of the things we substitute for God are not good or bad in and of themselves. They can be valuable and even commanded by God when they help us in our relationships with Him. They become despised by God when we turn them into substitutes for Him. Our human tendency is to turn to substitutes for Him, His presence, purposes, and ways. However:

- There is no substitute for life that comes from God.
- Only God can set the agenda for Kingdom work.
- We cannot accomplish Kingdom work in human ways.

MESSAGE NOTES: SUBSTITUTES FOR GOD

> **JEREMIAH 2:5-6A,8A,11,13** • ⁵This is what the Lord says:
> "What fault did your fathers find in me,
>   that they strayed so far from me?
> They followed worthless idols
>   and became worthless themselves.
> ⁶They did not ask, 'Where is the Lord,
>   who brought us up out of Egypt?
> ⁸The priests did not ask,
>   'Where is the Lord?'
>   Those who deal with the law did not
>   know me;
> ¹¹Has a nation ever changed its gods?
>   (Yet they are not gods at all.)
> But my people have exchanged their Glory
>   for worthless idols.
> ¹³"My people have committed two sins:
> They have forsaken me,
>   the spring of living water,
> and have dug their own cisterns,
>   broken cisterns that cannot hold water."

- There is no substitute for God.

- The biblical image is graphic: God is like an artesian well that comes from deep within the earth that never stops flowing. When we substitute for God, we start to dig out from a rock some kind of bowl that can hold water. The bowl itself is cracked. So when we come to drink, there's nothing to quench our thirst.

- God comes back to His people in every generation and says, I want you to go back to the original word that you had from Me.

> **MATTHEW 16:18** • "I will build my church, and the gates of Hades will not overcome it."

- If the gates of hell are prevailing, the problem is not with God; the problem is we are trying to trust in substitutes for God.

> **JOHN 6:44** • "No one can come to me unless the Father who sent me draws him, and I will raise him up at the last day. ⁴⁵It is written in the Prophets: 'They will all be taught by God.' Everyone who listens to the Father and learns from him comes to me."

- If we come to the place where we are going to trust in substitutes to draw people to God, God says, "I'll let you do it, but you'll have an empty cistern." You will have exchanged your glory for an idol. You will have exchanged the fountain of living water for that which cannot quench thirst.

- The more we trust in something other than God, the less we have of Him. We cannot have substitutes and God at the same time. If we trust in substitutes, we have the form but not the power.

> **ISAIAH 30:1-5** • ¹"Woe to the obstinate children," declares the Lord,
> "to those who carry out plans that are not mine, forming an alliance, but not by my Spirit, heaping sin upon sin;
> ²who go down to Egypt

without consulting me;
who look for help to Pharaoh's protection,
    to Egypt's shade for refuge.
³But Pharaoh's protection will be to your
    shame, Egypt's shade will bring you
    disgrace.
⁴Though they have officials in Zoan
    and their envoys have arrived in Hanes,
⁵everyone will be put to shame
    because of a people useless to them,
who bring neither help nor advantage,
    but only shame and disgrace."

ISAIAH 31:1 • Woe to those who go down to
    Egypt for help,
        who rely on horses,
    who trust in the multitude of their chariots
        and in the great strength of their horse
        men,
    but do not look to the Holy One of Israel,
        or seek help from the Lord.

• An idol is anything we turn to other than God.

• It is offensive to God when we turn to something else
  when He told us to turn to Him. God said, "You've
  just exchanged this for Me."

HEBREWS 10:31 • ³¹It is a dreadful thing to fall into the
hands of the living God.

• In Exodus 33:1-3, God gave His people a significant
  test.

EXODUS 33:1-3 • ¹Then the Lord said to
Moses, "Leave this place, you and the people
you brought up out of Egypt, and go up to the
land I promised on oath to Abraham, Isaac and
Jacob, saying, 'I will give it to your descendants.' ²I will send an angel before you and
drive out the Canaanites, Amorites, Hittites,
Perizzites, Hivites and Jebusites. ³Go up to the
land flowing with milk and honey. But I will

not go with you, because you are a stiff-necked people and I might destroy you on the way."

- If we don't know God and experience a relationship with Him, we don't have life. God is our life (Deut. 30: 19b-20).

- God intends for His people to trust exclusively in Him so that He can be glorified and revealed to a watching world.

> **JOHN 14:15-21** • [15]"If you love me, you will obey what I command. [16]And I will ask the Father, and he will give you another Counselor to be with you forever—[17]the Spirit of truth. The world cannot accept him, because it neither sees him nor knows him. But you know him, for he lives with you and will be in you. [18]I will not leave you as orphans; I will come to you. [19]Before long, the world will not see me anymore, but you will see me. Because I live, you also will live. [20]On that day you will realize that I am in my Father, and you are in me, and I am in you. [21]Whoever has my commands and obeys them, he is the one who loves me. He who loves me will be loved by my Father, and I too will love him and show myself to him."

- "It" (a program or method) has no power. Only God has power. We need more than "it"; we need God.

- Turn back to God. He will not fail you or forsake you. There is nothing to which God will call you that He will not enable you to accomplish.

- There is no life except the life that comes from God.

> **JAMES 4:4-7A** • [4]You adulterous people, don't you know that friendship with the world is hatred toward God? Anyone who chooses to be a friend of the world becomes an enemy of God. [5]Or do you think Scripture says without reason that the spirit he caused to live in us

envies intensely? ⁶But he gives us more grace. That is why Scripture says:

"God opposes the proud
but gives grace to the humble."
⁷Submit yourselves, then, to God.

QUESTIONS FOR GOD'S PEOPLE

1. How do you see God's glory in your life? in your church?
2. Does the community where God planted your church fear the God you serve? Why or why not?
3. Are you experiencing a form of religion without God's power?
4. Do you fear Satan more than you do God?
5. Is God the last place you turn or the first place you turn for direction?
6. Do people in the world speak more about our church or about the God of our church?
7. Read Exodus 33:1-3. Do you want success or the presence of God? Do you want (you fill in the blank) _____ or the presence of God?
8. Are we interpreting success for the presence of God?
9. Are we experiencing unrest because we have turned to things other than to God?

Have you, your family, or your church turned to substitutes for God? Complete the following activity to see.

INSTRUCTIONS: Read through the following list of possible substitutes. Ask God to reveal to you any thing, person, group, or activity that you have turned to as a substitute for Him, His presence, purposes, or ways. Remember that many of the things listed below are only "bad" when we substitute them for God. If God reveals any of these as substitutes, past or present, for which you need to repent, mark it on the line to the left of the item. Use the following letters to indicate for whom each item became a substitute:

S = Self   C = Church
F = Family   O = Other group

___ Trusting methods rather than trusting God.

___ Trusting programs rather than trusting God.

___ Trusting other people rather than trusting God.

___ Trusting organizations rather than trusting God.

___ Trusting people and political action rather than trusting God.

___ Trusting _____ rather than trusting God.

___ Substituting emotionalism for experiencing God's presence in worship.

___ Substituting religious ritual for experiencing God's presence in worship.

___ Substituting elaborate pageantry for experiencing God's presence in worship.

___ Substituting entertainment for experiencing God's presence in worship.

___ Substituting human traditions for experiencing God's presence in worship.

___ Substituting famous people for experiencing God's presence in worship.

___ Substituting _____ for experiencing God's presence in worship.

___ Spending so much time watching television that I do not have time for my relationship with God.

___ Spending so much time in my job or earning extra money that I do not have time for my relationship with God.

___ Spending so much time working in organizations that I do not have time for my relationship with God.

___ Spending so much time doing church-related work that I do not have time for my relationship with God.

___ Spending so much time taking care of the things I own (house, yard, cars, boats, gardens, and so on) that I do not have time for my relationship with God.

___ Spending so much time in recreational activities that I do not have time for my relationship with God.

___ Spending so much time _____ that I do not have time for my relationship with God.

___ Spending so much time as a church doing _____
_____ that our members
do not have time for their relationship with God.

___ Substituting Bible study and going through my prayer lists for a love relationship with God.

___ Substituting relationships with other people for a love relationship with God.

___ Being in love with the world and the things of the world rather than in love with God. Striving for riches rather than a relationship.

___ Looking for fullness of life in sexual relationships rather than looking to Him who is my life.

___ Looking to the futurists and sociologists to decide what kind of church we need for the future rather than looking to Christ who is Head of His church and who alone knows the future.

___ Looking to the books of men for guidance rather than looking to God's Word for guidance.

___ Focusing on a practical popular theology of spiritual gifts rather than being filled with the Holy Spirit.

___ Seeking the praise of people rather than the praise of God.

___ Refusing to offend people even when we offend a holy God in the process.

___ Relying on human reason instead of God's revelation.

SUBSTITUTES FOR GOD'S PURPOSES

___ Caring about numbers and goals instead of people.

___ Spending time and resources on self or our church but not spending time or resources to meet the needs of those around us who need our help.

___ Caring about people's physical condition but not caring about their spiritual condition.

___ Being content with church members who attend without any concern for or attempt to help the "sheep" who have gone astray or who are broken and hurting away from the "fold."

___ Being satisfied with the signs of "success" (budgets, buildings, baptisms, attendance, and so on) without the manifest presence and power of Almighty God.

____ Spending so much time inside the church building that we don't have time to care for the needs of the sick, naked, hungry, thirsty, or prisoner outside the church building.

____ Working hard at the ritual practice of religion but ignoring justice and mercy for the poor and oppressed.

____ Settling for a decision for "baptism" and church membership rather than being sure the person is a convert and a disciple.

SUBSTITUTES FOR GOD'S WAYS

____ Walking by sight doing only what we know we can do rather than walking by faith in the One who calls us to do it.

____ Marketing the church with advertising, promotion, and gimmicks rather than letting God reveal Himself through us to draw people to Himself.

____ Living by the letter of the Law rather than by the spirit of the Law.

____ Promoting ourselves rather than denying ourselves.

____ Living to die rather than dying to ourselves to live.

____ Living by the world's ways rather than by Kingdom ways.

Notes

World's Ways vs. Kingdom Ways

> **JOHN 15:10-11** • [10]"If you obey my commands, you will remain in my love, just as I have obeyed my Father's commands and remain in his love. [11]I have told you this so that my joy may be in you and that your joy may be complete."

- We have taken on the ways of the world and exchanged them for the ways of the Kingdom.

- God says one thing, and the world says another. We have to decide who is telling the truth.

> **MATTHEW 6:9-10** • [9]"This, then, is how you should pray:
> " 'Our Father in heaven,
> hallowed be your name,
> [10]your kingdom come,
> your will be done
> on earth as it is in heaven.' "

- If we depart from God's ways, the redemption of the world is at stake.

> **COLOSSIANS 1:13,26-27** • [13]For he has rescued us from the dominion of darkness and brought us into the kingdom of the Son he loves.
> [26]The mystery that has been kept hidden for ages and generations, but is now disclosed to the saints. [27]To them God has chosen to make known among the Gentiles the glorious riches of this mystery, which is Christ in you, the hope of glory.

- God's provision is to place His Son in you, then start to conform everything about you on the outside to look like the Person who is reigning and supreme on the inside.

- Christ in you does not only rule, He also serves. He is the Master Servant (see Isa. 53).

- We have made a fatal mistake if we choose the world's ways.

- You cannot keep magnifying yourself and your church over the affirmation of the lordship of Christ.

- Christ is the most important One in our church.

- The more you affirm God in your church, the more He is able to work through you.

> **COLOSSIANS 2:2-4,6-8** • ²My purpose is that they may be encouraged in heart and united in love, so that they may have the full riches of complete understanding, in order that they may know the mystery of God, namely, Christ, ³in whom are hidden all the treasures of wisdom and knowledge. ⁴I tell you this so that no one may deceive you by fine-sounding arguments.
>
> ⁶So then, just as you received Christ Jesus as Lord, continue to live in him, ⁷rooted and built up in him, strengthened in the faith as you were taught, and overflowing with thankfulness.
>
> ⁸See to it that no one takes you captive through hollow and deceptive philosophy, which depends on human tradition and the basic principles of this world rather than on Christ.

- Absolute wisdom and knowledge are found in Christ.

- We all need to know the difference between the world and the people of God.

- The world says you need to rule; the kingdom says you need to serve.

  > **JEREMIAH 11:2-3,6-8** • [2]"Listen to the terms of this covenant and tell them to the people of Judah and to those who live in Jerusalem. [3]Tell them that this is what the Lord, the God of Israel, says: 'Cursed is the man who does not obey the terms of this covenant.'"
  >
  > [6]The Lord said to me, "Proclaim all these words in the towns of Judah and in the streets of Jerusalem: 'Listen to the terms of this covenant and follow them. [7]From the time I brought your forefathers up from Egypt until today, I warned them again and again, saying, "Obey me." [8]But they did not listen or pay attention; instead, they followed the stubbornness of their evil hearts. So I brought on them all the curses of the covenant I had commanded them to follow but that they did not keep.'"

- God places His presence in His people and works mightily through them to redeem a lost world.

- Let us confess, "God, forgive us for believing a lie and rejecting the truth."

- God's Word is the most practical guide for ministry and mission for the people of God. The Bible is the textbook for guiding people to do the work and the will of God.

- The church needs to turn back to the Word of God, carefully looking to see what God is doing, mark down His ways, put them alongside the way the church is doing it, and make the adjustment, whatever it needs to be.

ISAIAH 55:8-13 • [8]"For my thoughts are not
your thoughts,
neither are your ways my ways,"
declares the Lord.
[9]"As the heavens are higher than the earth,
so are my ways higher than your ways
and my thoughts than your thoughts.
[10]As the rain and the snow
come down from heaven,
and do not return to it
without watering the earth
and making it bud and flourish,
so that it yields seed for the sower and
bread for the eater,
[11]so is my word that goes out from my mouth:
It will not return to me empty,
but will accomplish what I desire
and achieve the purpose for which
I sent it.
[12]You will go out in joy
and be led forth in peace;
the mountains and hills
will burst into song before you,
and all the trees of the field
will clap their hands.
[13]Instead of the thornbush will grow the pine
tree, and instead of briers the myrtle will
grow.
This will be for the Lord's renown,
for an everlasting sign,
which will not be destroyed."

QUESTIONS FOR GOD'S PEOPLE

1. Do you live more by Kingdom ways or the world's
ways?
2. Do you sense that your church functions more in
Kingdom ways or in the world's ways?

Complete the following activity to help you answer these
questions.

Instructions: Read the following list of contrasts between the world's ways and Kingdom ways. For each set evaluate your life with the assistance of the Holy Spirit to discern whether you live more by Kingdom ways or the world's. Rate your behavior patterns in column A on a scale of 1 to 10 depending on how close you are to the world's ways (1) or to Kingdom ways (10). Go through the list a second time and rate your church in column B on the same scale for those items that would apply to a church.

If you disagree with how the world's way or Kingdom way is stated, circle it and write it in your own words. Make sure Kingdom ways agree with Scripture.

A   B

_____ _____

1. Take oaths, swear by oath to indicate you are telling the truth.

_____ _____

Do not take oaths of any kind. Let your yes and no be truthful (see Matt. 5:34,37).

_____ _____

2. Get revenge on those who mistreat you.

_____ _____

Turn the other cheek and let God be your avenger (see Matt. 5:38-39).

_____ _____

3. Give only what is demanded by others or those in authority.

_____ _____

Give more than what is demanded (see Matt. 5:41).

_____ _____

4. Hate your enemy. Treat them the way they treat you.

_____ _____

Love your enemy. Do good to those who hate you (see Matt. 5:43-44; Luke 6:27-28).

_____ _____

5. Show off your religious activity in public.

_____ _____

Fast, pray, and give in secret (see Matt. 6:1-6; 6:16-18).

_____ _____

6. Hold a grudge. Don't show weakness by forgiving.

_____ _____

Forgive without limits (see Matt. 6:14-15; Mark 11:25).

7. Store up treasures on earth, save for a "rainy day." "The one with the most toys wins in the game of life."

   Store up treasures in heaven, not on the earth (see Matt. 6:19-21; Luke 12:21,32-34).

8. Try to serve God, things, money, and materialism.

   Serve God alone (see Matt. 6:24; Luke 16:9-13).

9. Strive for food and clothes and worry about tomorrow. Take care of the basics and then serve God.

   Seek first God's kingdom (rule) and don't worry about tomorrow—what you will eat and wear (see Matt. 6:25-34).

10. Point out the faults in others—especially the ones you yourself may secretly be guilty of.

    Judge yourself first and correct your own behavior before trying to help correct someone else (see Matt. 7:1-5).

11. Don't do any more for someone than he or she does for you. Treat others the way they treat you.

    Treat others the way you would like to be treated (see Matt. 7:12).

12. Sound religious. Hear and ignore God's Word.

    Hear and obey God's will, God's Word (see Matt. 7:24-27).

13. Love your family more than anyone. Give family wishes your first priority.

    Love Christ more than anyone. Give God's desires your first priority (see Matt. 8:21-22; 10:37).

14. Enlist, beg, plead, manipulate, and use guilt to secure workers for God's work.

    Pray for God to call and send laborers (see Matt. 9:37-38).

A B	

15. Give grudgingly, sparingly.

Give to God's work freely. (see Matt. 10:8; Luke 6:38).

16. Don't speak boldly about Christ. People may reject you or be offended.

Speak about Christ freely (see Matt. 10:17-33).

17. Affirm self. Look out for yourself. Take care of yourself. Hold on to what you have.

Deny self. Lose yourself for the Kingdom's sake. Die to self. Give yourself away (see Matt. 10:38-39; Luke 9:23-25; Matt. 16:24-25).

18. Pay attention to the well-being of the majority of church members and don't waste time on the strays. Let them come back when they get their lives right.

Go after even one sheep (church member) that has gone astray (see Matt. 18:10-14).

19. When things get tough in a marriage, get a divorce.

Don't divorce. Keep marriages (holy matrimony) together (see Matt. 19:3-11; 1 Cor. 7:10-11; Malachi 2:13-16).

20. Rule over others. Exercise the authority of your position. Throw your weight (influence) around to get your way.

Serve to be great. Be a slave to be first (see Matt. 20:25-28).

21. Expect others to serve you, to meet your needs.

Serve others as Christ did (see Matt. 20:28).

22. Treat the church as a business enterprise. Focus on religious externals.

Make God's house a house of prayer (see Matt. 21:13).

	A	B

23. Withhold resources (tithes and taxes) for use on yourself. Get out of paying taxes whenever you can.

Give to God what is God's and to the government what belongs to it (see Matt. 22:21).

24. Use moderation in your commitments to God. Don't be a religious fanatic. People won't like you, or they will think you are crazy.

Love God with all your heart, soul, mind, and strength (see Matt. 22:37).

25. Ignore your neighbor (anyone who has need of your help) especially when helping is inconvenient or costly to you.

Love your neighbor and demonstrate your love by meeting his or her needs no matter how inconvenient or costly (see Matt. 22:39; Luke 10:30-37).

26. Give only what you are willing to be a disciple. Set your own requirements.

Give up everything to be a disciple. Release all you have to His lordship (see Luke 14:34).

27. Plan what you want to do for God and ask Him to bless it.

Look to see where God is at work and join Him (see John 5:19-20).

28. Please yourself.

Please God (see John 5:30).

29. Advertise, market the church, use gimmicks to draw people to your church.

Depend on God to exalt Jesus and draw people to Himself (see John 6:44,65).

____ ____

30. Say whatever you want to say as you teach others.

____ ____

Speak only the words God gives you to say. Teach only those things He gives you to teach (see John 12:49-50).

31. Earn eternal life by your good works.

____ ____

Be justified with God by faith and receive His mercy and grace as a free gift (see Rom. 5:1; Gal. 2:15-20; Eph. 2:8-9).

32. Set your mind on whatever your sinful nature desires.

____ ____

Set your mind on what the Spirit desires (see Rom. 8:5).

33. In the church practice jealousy, quarreling, and division.

____ ____

In the church practice love and be united in mind and heart (see 1 Cor. 3:3).

34. Be proud that you are tolerant of openly sinful people.

____ ____

Be grieved over sin. Take church action against those who openly practice sin and thus defame the name of Christ (1 Cor. 5:1-12).

35. Depend on yourself, your abilities, and your resources.

____ ____

Depend on God (see 2 Cor. 1:9; Jer. 17:5,7; Ps. 20:7).

36. Live by sight. Attempt only what you know you can do.

____ ____

Live by faith. Please God by following Him even when you cannot see how it can be done (see 2 Cor. 5:7; Heb. 11:6).

37. Wage war against spiritual enemies the way the world wages war. Use human weapons and means.

____ ____

Wage war against spiritual enemies with spiritual weapons of divine power (see 2 Cor. 10:3-5).

38. Focus on keeping the letter of the law, keeping the rules, doing the right things.

    Focus on the spirit of the law that is revealed through a relationship with the Spirit of God (see 2 Cor. 3:6).

39. Be motivated by guilt or duty.

    Be motivated by the love of Christ (see 2 Cor. 5:14).

40. Form alliances with anyone who can benefit us.

    Be separate, not unequally yoked to unbelievers (see 2 Cor. 6:14,17).

41. Perform acts of the sinful nature: sexual immorality, impurity and debauchery; idolatry and witchcraft; hatred, discord, jealousy, fits of rage, selfish ambition, dissensions, factions and envy; drunkenness, and orgies.

    Demonstrate fruit of the Spirit: love, joy, peace, patience, kindness, goodness, faithfulness, gentleness and self-control (see Gal. 5:19-23).

42. If a Christian is caught in a sin: ignore it, gossip about it, reject him or her.

    Restore the sinful Christian gently being careful to not let yourself be tempted (see Gal. 6:1).

43. Look to humans for leadership of the church.

    Look to Christ for leadership of the church (see Eph. 1:22-23).

44. Seek access to God through men.

    Find direct access to the Father through Christ and through the Spirit (see Eph. 2:18).

45. Employees do only enough to get by and relate to their employers as adversaries.

    Employees obey their employers and serve them wholeheartedly as serving the Lord (see Eph. 6:5-8).

46. Employers try to get just as much out of employees as they can for as little cost as possible. They relate to employees as adversaries.

Employers take care of their employees and express their care as caring for the Lord Himself (see Eph. 6:9; Col. 4:1).

47. Grieve at the death of a loved one as one who has no hope for the future.

Live as a people with hope for the future when a loved one dies in Christ (see 1 Thess. 4:13-18).

48. Show favoritism. Give special attention to the rich and influential people. Treat them differently than you would the poor and common people.

Love your neighbor as yourself. Don't show favoritism or discriminate (see Jas. 2:1-11).

49. Keep man's traditions.

Obey God's commands (see Matt. 15:3-9).

50. "When in Rome, do as the Romans do." Become like the world. Fit in.

Don't let the world shape you into its mold. Let God transform you (see Rom. 12:1-2).

Unholy Living vs. Holy Living

HOLY: set apart to the service of God; spiritually pure.[1]

MESSAGE NOTES: UNHOLY LIVING VS. HOLY LIVING

• Never does a Christian have more of a sense of terror than when in the presence of Holy God and aware of the severity of his or her sin.

• There is a direct correlation between the understanding you have of God and the understanding you have of sin. A high view of God brings a high view of sin; a low view of God brings a low view of sin.

• To walk in the presence of a holy God and live an unholy life is spiritually impossible (see Isa. 6).

• Nobody can walk in fellowship with a holy God and not hear His heart cry to win a world to Himself.

> **LEVITICUS 11:44-45,47** • [44]I am the Lord your God; consecrate yourselves and be holy, because I am holy. Do not make yourselves unclean by any creature that moves about on the ground. [45]I am the Lord who brought you up out of Egypt to be your God; therefore be holy, because I am holy.
> [47]You must distinguish between the unclean and the clean.

> **PHILIPPIANS 4:8** • Finally, brothers, whatever is true, whatever is noble, whatever is right, whatever is pure, whatever is lovely, whatever is admirable—if anything is excellent or praise-worthy—think about such things.

- You cannot let the filth of television pass through your thoughts and remain clean in your mind. The two are not compatible.

- Make certain you distinguish between the clean and unclean.

> **LEVITICUS 10:10-11** • [10]You must distinguish between the holy and the common, between the unclean and the clean, [11]and you must teach the Israelites all the decrees the Lord has given them through Moses."

- Spiritual leaders and parents must teach the people of God the difference between the holy and the common.

> **MATTHEW 5:3-8**
> [3]"Blessed are the poor in spirit,
>   for theirs is the kingdom of heaven.
> [4]Blessed are those who mourn,
>   for they will be comforted.
> [5]Blessed are the meek,
>   for they will inherit the earth.
> [6]Blessed are those who hunger and thirst for
>   righteousness, for they will be filled.
> [7]Blessed are the merciful,
>   for they will be shown mercy.
> [8]Blessed are the pure in heart,
>   for they will see God.

> **HEBREWS 12:14** • Make every effort to live in peace with all men and to be holy; without holiness no one will see the Lord.

> **EZEKIEL 22:23-26,29-31** • [23]Again the word of the Lord came to me: [24]"Son of man, say to the land, 'You are a land that has had no rain or showers in the day of wrath.' [25]There is a conspiracy of her princes within her like a roaring lion tearing its prey; they devour people, take treasures and precious things and make many widows within her. [26]Her priests do violence to my law and profane my holy things; they do not

distinguish between the holy and the common; they teach that there is no difference between the unclean and the clean; and they shut their eyes to the keeping of my Sabbaths, so that I am profaned among them.

²⁹The people of the land practice extortion and commit robbery; they oppress the poor and needy and mistreat the alien, denying them justice.

³⁰"I looked for a man among them who would build up the wall and stand before me in the gap on behalf of the land so I would not have to destroy it, but I found none. ³¹So I will pour out my wrath on them and consume them with my fiery anger, bringing down on their own heads all they have done, declares the Sovereign Lord."

- We are now experiencing the pain of having departed from a holy God in our personal lives, marriages, children, grandchildren, the school system, and the financial condition of the nation. Society begins to crumble because the people of God, who were intended to be the instrument to redeem a world, are no longer of use to God.

- Our nation is increasingly saying that nothing is unholy.

- The people of God are no longer evidence that there is a difference between the holy and unholy.

- We are a generation of Christians that does not want to offend people or Satan, but we will offend God without any compunction at all.

- We have no fear of God.

- In the Bible, Satan never destroyed the people of God, but God did.

MALACHI 3:7 • "Return to me and I will return to you," says the Lord Almighty.

EZEKIEL 36:22-23,25-27 • [22]"Therefore say to the house of Israel, 'This is what the Sovereign Lord says: It is not for your sake, O house of Israel, that I am going to do these things, but for the sake of my holy name, which you have profaned among the nations where you have gone. [23]I will show the holiness of my great name, which has been profaned among the nations, the name you have profaned among them. Then the nations will know that I am the Lord, declares the Sovereign Lord, when I show myself holy through you before their eyes.

[25]" 'I will sprinkle clean water on you, and you will be clean; I will cleanse you from all your impurities and from all your idols. [26]I will give you a new heart and put a new spirit in you; I will remove from you your heart of stone and give you a heart of flesh. [27]And I will put my Spirit in you and move you to follow my decrees and be careful to keep my laws.' "

- The whole redemption of a lost world waits for our choosing to return to God.

- The call to salvation is a call for God's people to be on mission with Him reflecting Him to our world.

- The world is not coming to Jesus because they don't see anything in us they don't already have.

EPHESIANS 5:25-27 • [25]Christ loved the church and gave himself up for her [26]to make her holy, cleansing her by the washing with water through the word, [27]and to present her to himself as a radiant church, without stain or wrinkle or any other blemish, but holy and blameless.

JOHN 17:17-19 • [17]"Sanctify them by the truth; your word is truth. [18]As you sent me into the world, I have sent them into the world.

¹⁹For them I sanctify myself, that they too may be truly sanctified."

1 PETER 1:13-16 • ¹³Therefore, prepare your minds for action; be self-controlled; set your hope fully on the grace to be given you when Jesus Christ is revealed. ¹⁴As obedient children, do not conform to the evil desires you had when you lived in ignorance. ¹⁵But just as he who called you is holy, so be holy in all you do; ¹⁶for it is written: "Be holy, because I am holy."

QUESTIONS FOR GOD'S PEOPLE

1. Have you ever been so aware of God's holiness that you trembled at the sense of your sinfulness?

2. Would you say that your church treats the following as holy and dedicated to the Lord or as common? Write "H" for holy and "C" for common.

_____ a. The Lord's Day

_____ b. The Lord's name

_____ c. The Lord's house

_____ d. The Lord's Supper

_____ e. Baptism

_____ f. Marriage

_____ g. God's commands, decrees, laws

_____ h. Tithes and offerings

_____ i. The Scriptures

_____ j. The church

_____ k. Spiritual leaders

_____ l. All believers

3. Do you fear God? Does your church fear God? Does your community fear God? Does our nation fear God?

4. Which of these words from Scripture describe your church? Check all that apply.

❏ radiant

❏ without stain

❏ without wrinkle

❏ without blemish

❏ holy

❏ blameless

❏ pure

5. Do you consider your own body as holy and dedicated to God? Do you reflect the Holy Spirit who dwells in you? Read Romans 12:1-2.

6. Read the following Scriptures and circle the words or phrases that describe a holy life. Underline the words or phrases that describe an unholy life. As you read, ask the Lord to identify anything in your life that needs to change.

EPHESIANS 1:4 • For he chose us in him before the creation of the world to be holy and blameless in his sight.

EPHESIANS 5:3-4 • ³But among you there must not be even a hint of sexual immorality, or of any kind of impurity, or of greed, because these are improper for God's holy people. ⁴Nor should there be obscenity, foolish talk or coarse joking, which are out of place, but rather thanksgiving.

COLOSSIANS 1:21-22 • ²¹Once you were alienated from God and were enemies in your minds because of your evil behavior. ²²But now he has reconciled you by Christ's physical body through death to present you holy in his sight, without blemish and free from accusation.

1 THESSALONIANS 4:3-5,7-8 • ³It is God's will that you should be sanctified: that you should avoid sexual immorality; ⁴that each of you should learn to control his own body in a way that is holy and honorable, ⁵not in passionate lust like the heathen, who do not know God;

⁷For God did not call us to be impure, but to live a holy life. ⁸Therefore, he who rejects this instruction does not reject man but God, who gives you his Holy Spirit.

2 PETER 3:11,14 • ¹¹What kind of people ought you to be? You ought to live holy and godly lives.

¹⁴So then, dear friends, since you are looking forward to this, make every effort to be found spotless, blameless and at peace with him.

ISAIAH 8:13 • The Lord Almighty is the one you are to regard as holy, he is the one you are to fear, he is the one you are to dread.

ISAIAH 48:17 • This is what the Lord says— your Redeemer, the Holy One of Israel: "I am the Lord your God, who teaches you what is best for you, who directs you in the way you should go."

7. Read the following Scriptures about God's holy name. Do you treat God's name as holy, or do you profane His name?

> **LEVITICUS 19:12**
> **LEVITICUS 22:31-33**
> **MALACHI 1:10-14**

8. Read the following Scriptures about the Sabbath and answer the questions. Ask God to guide you to know what He desires regarding the Lord's Day (our Sabbath).

> **MATTHEW 12:7-8,11-12**
> **MARK 2:27-28**

- Is God more interested in sacrifice or mercy? Is He more interested in your keeping the letter of the law or the spirit of the law?
- Who is Lord of the Sabbath?
- What is lawful to do on the Sabbath?
- Who was the Sabbath made for?

> **GENESIS 2:3**
> **EXODUS 20:8-11**

- Why did God set the Sabbath aside as a holy day of rest?
- Have those reasons changed?

EXODUS 31:13-14,16-17
EZEKIEL 20:12-14
EZEKIEL 20:20

- What is the Sabbath a sign of?
- How lasting is this covenant agreement between God and His people?

NEHEMIAH 10:31
NEHEMIAH 13:22
JEREMIAH 17:21-24,27

- What are some of the activities that were not permitted on the Sabbath?
- How did God respond to His people when they were stiff-necked and would not listen or respond to His discipline about the keeping of the Sabbath?

ISAIAH 58:13—59:2

- What does God ask His people not to do on the Sabbath?
- What is God's promise for keeping the Sabbath day holy?
- What are the consequences of disregarding God's command about the Sabbath?
- What can we do to help each other use the Lord's Day (our Sabbath) as a time to renew fellowship with God?
- What are some appropriate ways for us to use the Lord's Day?
- How can you keep the Lord's Day holy—set apart for Him?

---

[1] *Webster's New Collegiate Dictionary* (Springfield, Mass.: G. & C. Merriam Co., 1981), 542.

Broken Relationships vs. Unity in the Body

- God works through His people to call them to unity rather than brokenness.

- When the people of God become broken and separated from each other, their brokenness separates them from God. It is spiritually impossible to be right with God and wrong with a fellow Christian.

    JOHN 13:34-35 • [34]"A new command I give you: Love one another. As I have loved you, so you must love one another. [35]By this all men will know that you are my disciples, if you love one another."

- The more our relationships with one another are broken, the less He is able to redeem a lost world. God holds us accountable.

- God Himself dwells in your brother. You are treating God the same way you treat your brother or sister.

    JOHN 13:20 • "I tell you the truth, whoever accepts anyone I send accepts me; and whoever accepts me accepts the one who sent me."

- Your whole spiritual life with God is affected by how you respond to your brother or sister in Christ.

- A person in the world tries to be reconciled; the Christian *is* reconciled.

1 JOHN 3:14 • We know that we have passed from death to life, because we love our brothers. Anyone who does not love remains in death.

• The real test is whether you can love your fellow Christian for whom Christ died and in whom He now dwells. Your love for Jesus will cause you to love your fellow Christian.

1 JOHN 3:16 • This is how we know what love is: Jesus Christ laid down his life for us. And we ought to lay down our lives for our brothers.

1 JOHN 4:7-12 • [7]Dear friends, let us love one another, for love comes from God. Everyone who loves has been born of God and knows God. [8]Whoever does not love does not know God, because God is love. [9]This is how God showed his love among us: He sent his one and only Son into the world that we might live through him. [10]This is love: not that we loved God, but that he loved us and sent his Son as an atoning sacrifice for our sins. [11]Dear friends, since God so loved us, we also ought to love one another. [12]No one has ever seen God; but if we love one another, God lives in us and his love is made complete in us.

• Our unity with Him and with each other is God's basis for calling a whole world to know that He loves them and sent His Son for them.

JOHN 17:20-23 • [20]"My prayer is not for them alone. I pray also for those who will believe in me through their message, [21]that all of them may be one, Father, just as you are in me and I am in you. May they also be in us so that the world may believe that you have sent me. [22]I have given them the glory that you gave me, that they may be one as we are one: [23]I in them and you in me. May they be brought to com-

plete unity to let the world know that you sent
me and have loved them even as you have
loved me."

• How can you tell if you have departed from the relationship with God? Look at how you treat other
Christians.

• As you love one another you demonstrate your love for
Christ.

• Your love relationship with Christ determines your relationship with the Father.

• Your relationship with the Father determines your abili-
ty to be involved with Him in world redemption.

QUESTIONS FOR GOD'S PEOPLE

1. Do you or does your church have any broken relationships that require forgiveness, reconciliation, or restitu-
tion? Consider these relationships:

• Relationship between you and your spouse
• Relationship between you and an ex-spouse
• Relationship between you and your parent or you
and your child
• Relationship between your family and another family
• Relationship between you and a relative
• Relationship between you and a neighbor
• Relationship between you and an acquaintance
• Relationship between you and a friend
• Relationship between you and a Christian brother or
sister
• Relationship between you and a fellow employee
• Relationship between you and a business partner or
associate
• Relationship between your church and another
church, group, or individual
• Relationship between your denomination and another
denomination or group
• Relationship between your ethnic group and another
ethnic group

Ask God to guide you in knowing what is required for reconciliation and when and how to go about being reconciled. For family, church, and other group-type relationships, consult with the others as you seek to be reconciled. See if others agree with your evaluation about the broken relationship. Then pray together and examine the Scriptures to see how God would have you be reconciled.

2. How does your relationship with other Christians reflect your love relationship with God? Complete the following activity to see what God has to say.

Instructions: Read the following Scriptures from 1 John and meditate on the questions that follow. Ask God to reveal to you the nature of your relationship to Him. Ask Him to reveal any and every relationship you have with brothers and sisters in Christ that is not a right, healthy, and loving relationship. Keep in mind throughout that "brother" refers to other Christians—not only Christians in your church but anyone of any denomination who has experienced new birth in Jesus Christ.

◆ **Our Fellowship Is with the Father and His Son**

> 1 JOHN 1:3 • We proclaim to you what we have seen and heard, so that you also may have fellowship with us. And our fellowship is with the Father and with his Son, Jesus Christ.

• Do you have fellowship—an intimate and personal love relationship—with God the Father and with His Son, Jesus Christ?

◆ **Our Fellowship with God Is Reflected in Our Fellowship with One Another**

> 1 JOHN 1:7 • But if we walk in the light, as he is in the light, we have fellowship with one another, and the blood of Jesus, his Son, purifies us from all sin.

• Do you have an intimate and personal love relationship—fellowship—with your brothers and sisters in Christ?

- Are you walking in light as He is in the light or are you walking in darkness and trying to call it light?

◆ **We Can Check Our Love for God by Evaluating Our Love for Our Brother**

> 1 JOHN 3:10-11 • [10]This is how we know who the children of God are and who the children of the devil are: Anyone who does not do what is right is not a child of God; nor is anyone who does not love his brother.
> [11]This is the message you heard from the beginning: We should love one another.

- Do you have a God-like love for your brothers and sisters in Christ? Does that love reflect these qualities: patient, kind, not envious, not boastful, not proud but humble, not rude, not self-seeking, not easily angered, keeping no record of wrongs, not delighting in evil, rejoicing in truth, protecting, trusting, hoping, and persevering? (1 Cor. 13:4-7)

If these words do not describe your love for others, God sets another plumb line by which you need to measure your life:

> 1 JOHN 4:7-8 • [7]Dear friends, let us love one another, for love comes from God. Everyone who loves has been born of God and knows God. [8]Whoever does not love does not know God, because God is love.

- Is the love of God flowing through your life to others?
- Are there members of the body of Christ that you hate?

> 1 JOHN 2:9-11 • [9]Anyone who claims to be in the light but hates his brother is still in the darkness. [10]Whoever loves his brother lives in the light, and there is nothing in him to make him stumble. [11]But whoever hates his brother is in the darkness and walks around in the darkness; he does not know where he is going, because the darkness has blinded him.

- Are you saying to yourself, "Well, you just don't know the brothers and sisters in Christ that I know. I love God, but I just can't love them"?

> **1 JOHN 4:20-21** • [20]If anyone says, "I love God," yet hates his brother, he is a liar. For anyone who does not love his brother, whom he has seen, cannot love God, whom he has not seen. [21]And he has given us this command: Whoever loves God must also love his brother.

How you love your brother or sister is a good indicator of your relationship with God. If you consistently cannot get along with your fellow Christians, that may be an indicator of a deeper problem. It may indicate that you are still dead in transgressions and sins. Ask God to be the Great Physician and reveal the truth of your relationship with Him.

> **1 JOHN 3:14-15** • [14]We know that we have passed from death to life, because we love our brothers. Anyone who does not love remains in death. [15]Anyone who hates his brother is a murderer, and you know that no murderer has eternal life in him.

> **1 JOHN 4:11-12** • [11]Dear friends, since God so loved us, we also ought to love one another. [12]No one has ever seen God; but if we love one another, God lives in us and his love is made complete in us.

> **1 JOHN 5:1-3** • [1]Everyone who believes that Jesus is the Christ is born of God, and everyone who loves the father loves his child as well. [2]This is how we know that we love the children of God: by loving God and carrying out his commands. [3]This is love for God: to obey his commands. And his commands are not burdensome.

Here is God's plumb line for love:

> **1 JOHN 3:16-17** • [16]This is how we know

what love is: Jesus Christ laid down his life for us. And we ought to lay down our lives for our brothers. [17]If anyone has material possessions and sees his brother in need but has no pity on him, how can the love of God be in him?

- Do you know of brothers and sisters in Christ who have needs that can be met with financial or material possessions?
- Are you demonstrating your love by your actions and not just with your mouth?

1 JOHN 3:18 • Dear children, let us not love with words or tongue but with actions and in truth.

OTHER SCRIPTURES ABOUT RELATIONSHIPS

MATTHEW 5:23-24
MATTHEW 6:14-15
MATTHEW 18:21-22
MATTHEW 18:15-17
1 CORINTHIANS 1:10
EPHESIANS 4:26-27
HEBREWS 12:14-15
JOHN 17:20-23

A Corporate Prayer of Repentance
ADAPTED FROM DANIEL 9:4-19

[4]"O Lord, the great and awesome God, who keeps his covenant of love with all who love him and obey his commands, [5]we have sinned and done wrong. We have been wicked and have rebelled; we have turned away from your commands and laws. [6]We have not listened to your servants the prophets, who spoke in your name to our kings, our princes and our fathers, and to all the people of the land.

[7]"Lord, you are righteous, but this day we are covered with shame . . . because of our unfaithfulness to you. [8]O Lord, we and our [leaders] and our fathers are covered with shame because we have sinned against you. [9]The Lord our God is merciful and forgiving, even though we have rebelled against him; [10]we have not obeyed the Lord our God or kept the laws he gave us through his servants the prophets. [11][We all have] transgressed your law and turned away, refusing to obey you.

"Therefore the curses and sworn judgments written in the Law of Moses, the servant of God, have been poured out on us, because we have sinned against you. [12]You have fulfilled the words spoken against us and against our rulers by bringing upon us great disaster. . . . [13]Just as it is written in the Law of Moses, all this disaster has come upon us, yet we have not sought the favor of the Lord our God by turning from our sins and giving attention to your truth. [14]The Lord did not hesitate to bring the disaster upon us, for the Lord our God is righteous in everything he does; yet we have not obeyed him.

[15]"Now, O Lord our God, who brought your people out of Egypt with a mighty hand and who made for yourself a name that endures to this day, we have sinned, we have done wrong. [16]O Lord, in keeping with all your righteous acts, turn away your anger and your wrath

from [us]. Our sins and the iniquities of our fathers have made [us] an object of scorn to all those around us.

[17]"Now, our God, hear the prayers and petitions of your servant. For your sake, O Lord, look with favor on your desolate sanctuary. [18]Give ear, O God, and hear; open your eyes and see the desolation [in this place] that bears your Name. We do not make requests of you because we are righteous, but because of your great mercy. [19]O Lord, listen! O Lord, forgive! O Lord, hear and act! For your sake, O my God, do not delay, because . . . your people bear your Name."

Notes